BOSTON
THE CITY AT A GLANCE

Longfellow Bridge
Known as the 'salt and pepper sha[...]
due to the shape of its central tow[...]
1906 artery linking Boston and Ca[...]
was designed by Edmund M Wheel[...]

Hatch Memorial Shell
Located slap bang on the river, this outdoor
venue dates from 1941, and now plays host
to concerts, notably by the Boston Pops.
10 Storrow Memorial Drive, T 617 626 4970

TD Banknorth Garden
Home to both the Boston Bruins hockey team
and the Boston Celtics basketball team, this
1995 stadium is also a major concert venue.
See p092

Massachusetts State House
Designed by architect Charles Bulfinch
and opened in 1798, the State House stands
as a symbol of colonial-era grandeur.
See p064

Boston Common
The equivalent of New York's Central Park,
Boston Common is the city's green lung,
and the place where its myriad immigrant
communities mix and mingle.

Trinity Church
Once monumental, now dwarfed, this
Romanesque church dates from 1877, and
remains the city's main house of worship.
See p013

John Hancock Tower
Completed in 1976, IM Pei and Henry Cobb's
towering 60-storey Back Bay landmark is still
the tallest building in town.
See p068

INTRODUCTION

THE CHANGING FACE OF THE URBAN SCENE

Even though it is older – and more beautiful – than New York, Boston has always felt second tier when compared to its urban rival 320km to the south. Boston evokes a genteel sophistication that has resulted in its unrivalled status as the most European of US cities. But it is fast transforming from quaint to cool thanks to a wave of reinvention started by the Big Dig, which buried four miles of elevated highway and opened up vast tracts of land for new uses. Manageable in size and easy-going, Boston also has world-class museums and universities and a booming contemporary art scene, while its innovative restaurants pair Yankee traditionalism with European and Asian flavours. High finance and high-tech continue to thrive, and every aspect of city life benefits from the infusion of intellect and vitality brought by an ever-changing population.

Districts like the South End have gone from no-go zones to chic destinations filled with inventive eateries and shops, while Fort Point Channel is emerging as Boston's answer to NYC's SoHo, with its eye-catching loft conversions and landmark architecture. Even historic Beacon Hill is seeing new hotels blossom among the elegant colonial-era houses. Further out, areas such as Dorchester and Jamaica Plain are experiencing an influx of creative types and a happening gay scene. Back in the North End, Italian dominance is giving way to a more multicultural vibe. Boston has a fresh new face and is proving that old cities can learn new tricks.

ESSENTIAL INFO
FACTS, FIGURES AND USEFUL ADDRESSES

TOURIST OFFICE
Convention & Visitors Bureau
Suite 105
2 Copley Place
T 617 536 4100
bostonusa.com

TRANSPORT
Car hire
Hertz
30 Park Plaza
T 617 338 1500
hertz.com
Avis
202 Porter Street
T 617 563 500
avis.com
Public Transport
Massachusetts Bay Transport Authority
T 800 392 6100
mbta.com
Taxis
Boston Cab
T 617 536 3200
City Cab
T 617 536 5100

EMERGENCY SERVICES
Emergencies
T 911
24-hour pharmacy
CVS
587 Boylston Street
T 617 437 8414
cvs.com

CONSULATES
British Consulate-General
Suite 1500
1 Memorial Drive
T 617 245 4500
britainusa.com

MONEY
American Express
1 State Street
T 617 723 8400
travel.americanexpress.com

POSTAL SERVICES
Post Office
25 Dorchester Avenue
T 617 654 5302
Shipping
UPS
198 Tremont Street
T 617 426 3039
ups.com

BOOKS
The Big Dig by Dan McNichol and Andy Ryan (Silver Lining Books)
The Last Hurrah by Edwin O'Connor (Little, Brown)
The Scarlet Letter by Nathaniel Hawthorne (Penguin Classics)

WEBSITES
Architecture
iboston.org
Newspaper
boston.com

COST OF LIVING
Taxi from Boston Logan International Airport to city centre
£13.50
Cappuccino
£1.30
Packet of cigarettes
£3.25
Daily newspaper
£0.40
Bottle of champagne
£35

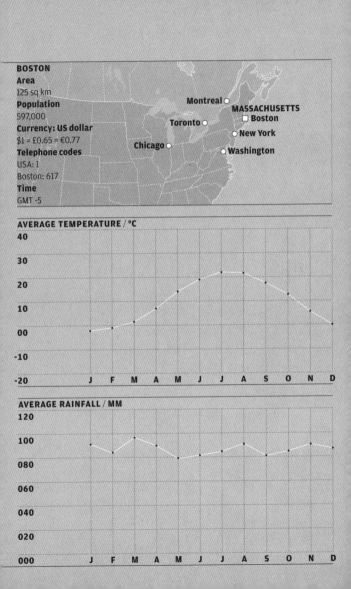

BOSTON
Area
125 sq km
Population
597,000
Currency: US dollar
$1 = £0.65 = €0.77
Telephone codes
USA: 1
Boston: 617
Time
GMT -5

Montreal
MASSACHUSETTS
Toronto   □ Boston
New York
Chicago
Washington

AVERAGE TEMPERATURE / °C

| | J | F | M | A | M | J | J | A | S | O | N | D |
40
30
20
10
00
-10
-20

AVERAGE RAINFALL / MM

120
100
080
060
040
020
000

| J | F | M | A | M | J | J | A | S | O | N | D |

NEIGHBOURHOODS

THE AREAS YOU NEED TO KNOW AND WHY

To help you navigate the city, we've chosen the most interesting districts (see below and the map inside the back cover) and colour-coded our featured venues, according to their location; those venues that are outside these areas are not coloured.

CAMBRIDGE

Actually a separate city just north of the Charles River, Cambridge was founded in 1630 and can boast two world-famous universities in Harvard (see p078) and the Massachusetts Institute of Technology (MIT; see p065, p070 and p074). It is a highly des-res district of spacious private homes and elegant colonial architecture.

DOWNTOWN

Landmarks include the skyscraper-filled waterfront, One International Place (see p076) and the 1849 Custom House (3 McKinley Square, T 617 310 6300). In the centre, Chinatown heaves with eateries and small businesses, while Faneuil Hall (see p012) is on the northern tip.

FORT POINT CHANNEL

This warren of brick warehouses from the late-19th and early-20th centuries lay dormant after WWII, until renovation began in the millennium. Now, shops, restaurants (see p042) and commercial spaces arrive weekly in a 'hood that also houses The Institute of Contemporary Art (see p072).

FENWAY

Home to Back Bay Fens park, this area is famous for cultural and leisure attractions, including the Boston Red Sox stadium (see p089), the Museum of Fine Arts (465 Huntington Avenue, T 617 267 9300) – in the midst of a Foster + Partners expansion – and the clubs on Landsdowne Street.

BACK BAY

'Rich, prosperous and monotonous' was how Henry James described Back Bay in 1909, by then a bastion of Boston's bourgeoisie. Its grand boulevards were modelled on Haussmann's Paris, and the enclave remains posh – though its main retail corridor, Newbury Street (see p086 and p087), has been overrun by big names.

SOUTH END

This area encompasses African-American, gay and Hispanic communities, and is filled with shops, such as the boutique Hudson (see p083), and classy restaurants, such as Aquitaine (see p045). Historically less wealthy than Back Bay, its townhouses and 11 parks now lure a new-moneyed crowd.

BEACON HILL

This suburb is the long-time home of the city's élite, who continue to occupy neo-Georgian, Federalist-style houses on cobblestoned streets lined with iron lanterns. Other draws are Massachusetts State House (see p064) at the peak and the tony shopping on Charles Street.

NORTH END

Boston's oldest neighbourhood is so ancient that it houses Paul Revere's circa-1680 'salt box'-styled home (see p009). At first the area filled with Irish immigrants, then the Italians moved in. Still Boston's Little Italy, its restaurants, bakeries and traditional social clubs cluster on Hanover Street.

LANDMARKS

THE SHAPE OF THE CITY SKYLINE

As the seat of the New England cultural, commercial and political élite for around four centuries, it's no surprise that Boston has its share of landmarks dating back to pre-Revolutionary times. They range from the historic – The Paul Revere House (19 North Square, T 617 523 2338), built around 1680 – to 19th-century masterpieces, such as Boston Public Library (700 Boylston Street, T 617 536 5400) and the Museum of Fine Arts (465 Huntington Avenue, T 617 267 9300), and 20th-century brutalism, such as City Hall (see p014). Indeed, the city's landmarks are as eclectic as its ever-expanding population, which reflects waves of immigration from Britain, France and eventually postwar Europe and Asia.

The city owes much of its distinctive look to its geography. First built along a trio of hills, central Boston is a fist-shaped peninsula surrounded on three sides by the Charles River and the harbour. The resulting usable land mass was small, but this was rectified by massive marsh drainage in the mid-19th century and citywide landfill schemes. Thanks to the recently completed Big Dig project, which buried the city's traffic-clogged elevated Central Artery, there are now new tracts of city-centre space available for future landmarks. Visitors can see the major sights in a day, taking in the towers in Downtown and Back Bay, the sports must-sees in Fenway and then the colonial-era beauties along Beacon Hill.
For full addresses, see Resources.

Citgo sign

With its prime location overlooking Fenway Park (see p089) – home of the Boston Red Sox – the Citgo Sign would appear to be as all-American as, well, baseball. Which is rather ironic, as the energy company is now owned by the Venezuelan government – aka Hugo Chávez. Nonetheless, the illuminated 'trimark' design remains one of Boston's most potent symbols, losing none of its lustre since its 1940 debut. Lit by thousands of energy-efficient LEDs, the 18 sq m sign is New England's largest but has never been officially declared a historic landmark. Even though the Chávez controversy has died down, many of the city's conservative politicians would welcome the sign's removal as a protest against the Venezuelan government's ongoing anti-American sentiments.
Kenmore Square, citgo.com

Faneuil Hall

This is Boston's most important gathering point – for shopping and eating – and has been since it was built in 1742. Patriotically known as The Cradle of Liberty, it was the scene of inspirational orations by Samuel Adams in the 1760s and 1770s – the beginnings of the rebellion that was to lead to America's independence. The original hall, funded by merchant Peter Faneuil, was renovated in 1806 by celebrated local architect Charles Bulfinch, who created its elegant cupola, light-filled arcades, columns and red-brick façade. Today, it is just one of many attractions in the Faneuil Hall Marketplace complex, which includes Quincy Market, North Market and South Market.

T 617 523 1300, faneuilhallmarketplace.com

Trinity Church

Set in Copley Square, this church was designed by Henry Hobson Richardson and completed in 1877 and is widely considered to be his most monumental building. Resoundingly Romanesque, its massive arches, grand towers and red clay roof marked a radical departure for American ecclesiastical design at the time. Along with its 64m-high central tower, Trinity Church is defined by a series of elaborate stained-glass windows, and the whole massive structure is anchored into the muddy wetlands by 4,500 wooden piles. The church remains the city's most important house of worship, and boasts a world-class choir.
206 Clarendon Street, T 617 536 0944,
trinitychurchboston.org

City Hall

Kallmann McKinnell and Knowles' 1969
brutalist City Hall exudes little warmth,
with its angular concrete façade and
red-brick plaza. While many politicians
are advocating selling off the prime real
estate, civic leaders are considering
granting the building landmark status.
An American Institute of Architects poll
ranked it the sixth best in US history.
1 City Hall Square

HOTELS

WHERE TO STAY AND WHICH ROOMS TO BOOK

Boston has enjoyed a hotel boom over the past five years with the opening of new boutiques and five-stars, as well as renovations of its grandes dames. The much-anticipated Mandarin Oriental (776 Boylston Street, T 617 535 8888) opened in 2008, with the city's top hotel spa among its attractions. And in the Fort Point Channel and Downtown districts a trio of exec-friendly luxury hotels have landed: the InterContinental (see p021), the Westin (425 Summer Street, T 617 532 4600) and the Renaissance (606 Congress Street, T 617 338 4111). All make the most of their harbour location and proximity to the city's new Convention & Exhibition Center.

Meanwhile, also in central Boston, The Liberty Hotel (overleaf) debuted in 2007 in a former jail, the Four Seasons (200 Boylston Street, T 617 338 4400) has had a facelift and California's boutique chain, Kimpton Hotels & Restaurants, opened its sleek Nine Zero (see p020) just steps away from the XV Beacon (see p022), which has offered expert service and haute cuisine since 1999. India's Taj Hotels spent millions revamping the former Ritz-Carlton, and rebranded it as the Taj (15 Arlington Street, T 617 536 5700), while the nearby The Fairmont Copley Plaza (opposite) underwent a similar makeover. There are also freshly decorated rooms across the river in The Charles Hotel (see p024), which was renovated in 2006, and is where Harvard's who's who like to check in.
For full addresses and room rates, see Resources.

The Fairmont Copley Plaza

Perched on a corner of Copley Square, The Fairmont has held a privileged place in Boston's hotel scene since debuting in 1912. A £18.8m renovation of the 383-room property saw the launch of Fairmont Gold, the Copley's hotel-within-a-hotel club. With its location and traditional 'palace hotel' aesthetic, The Fairmont offers little of the contemporary cool of its five-star competitors, but it doesn't try to. It is all about old-world splendour: frescoed walls, wood panelling, marble floors, sun-drenched skylights and lots of gold. This luxurious aesthetic is very evident in the Presidential Suite (above). Best of all though is the Oak Room – a traditional steakhouse with a good raw bar. It's consistently voted the best in town. *138 St James Avenue, T 617 267 5300, fairmont.com/copleyplaza*

The Liberty Hotel

It took a cool £83m to convert Charles Street Jail into The Liberty Hotel. Opened at the western end of Beacon Hill in 2007, the hotel has retained its 1851 granite façade, while adding 300 rooms, a gym, two bars and a pair of restaurants. At its core is the original atrium, now towering over the Clink bar, which overflows with Bostonians at the weekend; the atrium also has seating areas on the upper levels (above). Most of the rooms are in the newly built wing, and technology reigns supreme with high-definition TVs, VoIP telephones and iPod docks all present. Although several rooms have views of the Charles, the 18 in the original jail are the real steals – especially the ones with city views from floor-to-ceiling windows.
215 Charles Street, T 617 224 4000, libertyhotel.com

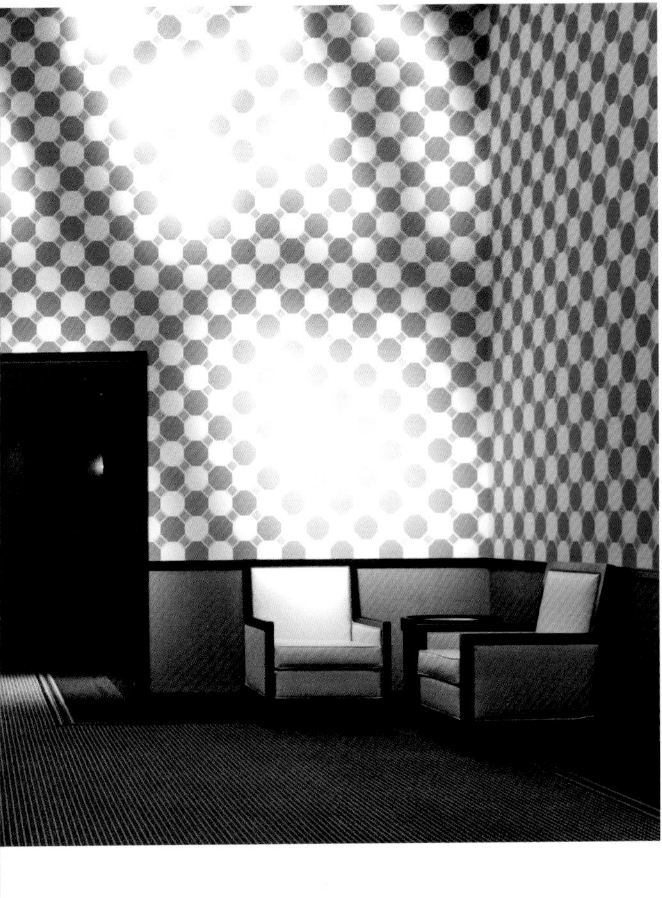

Nine Zero Hotel

Operated by San Francisco 'indie' Kimpton Hotels & Restaurants, Nine Zero sits on the top of Beacon Hill – at the start of the Freedom Trail and a stroll from Boston Common and the financial district. Hidden behind a red-brick and limestone exterior, its 190 rooms come in three categories: Deluxe, Premier and Premier with View, with the last having large windows that offer spectacular city vistas. Plump for the soaring Cloud Nine Penthouse Suite (above) for the ultimate in high living. The hotel is geared towards business travellers and has a tasty steakhouse, KO Prime (see p056), to tempt expense-accounters. It is also one of the most pet-friendly hotels in town, offering dog-sitting, walking and grooming services. *90 Tremont Street, T 617 772 5800, ninezero.com*

InterContinental

Within walking distance of South Station, this 424-room behemoth is aimed at both business and leisure travellers, with sprawling meeting spaces for the former, an elegant spa, gym and indoor lap pool for the latter, and classy furniture in the rooms for both. There is a strong emphasis on food, with options including a tasty Provençal restaurant, Miel; bar RumBa for tropical cocktails; and a sushi and tequila bar called Sushi-Teq. The best rooms are in the North Tower with harbour views – or opt for a sleek Superior Suite (above).
510 Atlantic Avenue, T 617 747 1000, intercontinentalboston.com

XV Beacon

When it opened in 1999, the XV Beacon was Boston's first true bijou boutique. Housed in a 10-storey Beaux Arts building, the hotel is an ode to style and technology, from the chic lobby (above) to the 60 unfussy rooms and complimentary chauffeur service. Though the rooms are on the small side — it's wise to go for a more spacious Studio Room (right) — they're reached by a charming 1903 cage elevator and are decked out with stainless-steel gas fireplaces and huge beds, some four-poster. Bathrooms have their own TVs, and minibars stock everything from Krug and Opus One to chilled cucumber eye-cream. The hotel has one of Boston's hottest restaurants too — the clubby Mooo (T 617 670 2515), which marries hearty, inventive Yankee fare with an extensive wine cellar.

15 Beacon Street, T 617 670 1500, xvbeacon.com

The Charles Hotel
Bill Clinton and the Dalai Lama have
both stayed in this neo-Shaker-styled
pad off Harvard Square. It is formal but
not fussy, with a classy lobby (pictured)
and 294 simply furnished rooms. Use
of the Wellbridge Athletic Club, a heritage
jazz bar and the restaurant Rialto (see
p048) pull in the parents and professors.
*1 Bennett Street, T 617 864 1200,
charleshotel.com*

Clarendon Square Inn

Capped by a 24-hour rooftop hot tub with panoramic city-centre views, the Clarendon Square Inn is Boston's most scenic small hotel and the only place to stay in the heart of the hip South End area. Owners Stephen Gross and Michael Selbst have added a strong dose of luxury while retaining the 19th-century feel of this townhouse B&B, which took almost a year to renovate. It has a mere three rooms, and only a small sign on its Victorian façade hints at the hospitality inside. Much of the original elegance is still in evidence, and has been accented by period-style furnishings and intimate, gracious service. Book the heavenly Clarendon Suite (above and right) for the ultimate New England experience. There is no restaurant on site, though the best of South End dining is on the doorstep.
198 W Brookline Street, T 617 536 2229, clarendonsquare.com

The Ritz-Carlton

Popular for its city-centre location, The Ritz-Carlton opened in 2001, and is the city's only real rival to the Four Seasons (see p016). However, both seem to have carved out their own niche: whereas the Four Seasons attracts a quiet, old-monied set, The Ritz-Carlton's glass-and-steel décor draws a younger, more glamorous and newly rich clientele. The hotel was given a £6m makeover in 2008 to create a new-look lobby, expanded Club Floor and more contemporary rooms (think Bang & Olufsen sound system and subtle fruity colours). Its Luxury Park View Suites and Presidential Suite (above) are very grand, while the hotel also features two restaurants and an excellent collection of contemporary New England art.
10 Avery Street, T 617 574 7100, ritzcarlton.com

The Beacon Hill Hotel

You really can't beat The Beacon Hill Hotel for its location, right where bustling Charles Street meets quaint Chestnut Street. Installed in two mid-19th-century townhouses with red-brick façades and white shutters, this 13-room hideaway is something of a chic oasis. The rooms are not grand, but are comfortable and cosy, and come with 21st-century essentials, such as flat-screen TVs and high-speed internet. Our favourite is the warm-toned and classic-styled Jacobs Suite (above and right). Owners Peter and Cecilia Rait previously ran a restaurant in Lisbon, and this is reflected in their ground-floor 76-seater Beacon Hill Bistro, which offers a fine selection of European-influenced dishes such as baked croque madame and braised Yorkshire pork shoulder with new carrots and cider raisin sauce.

25 Charles Street, T 617 723 7575, beaconhillhotel.com

24 HOURS

SEE THE BEST OF THE CITY IN JUST ONE DAY

Few neighbourhoods better symbolise Boston's resurgence than the South End, and a snapshot of the city can be garnered from a stroll around its charming streets. Once unfashionable, the area has bounced back by using its reputation for tolerance to lure creative types. Compact and bijou, it is stuffed with Victorian row houses, residential lofts and artists' studios. The studios are the attraction on the SoWa Art Walk (sowaartwalk.com) – a festival in late May, when the galleries and studios south of Washington Street open to the public. The buildings at 450 and 500 Harrison Avenue have the most compelling exhibits, and can be visited on the first Friday of every month during summer as well.

Start your day as Bostonians have for decades with breakfast at a diner such as Charlie's (opposite). Use the South End and Back Bay as your base to discover the Newbury Street art institutions, including the Barbara Krakow Gallery (see p037), and the shops of Union Park, such as Hudson (see p083). Also fit in a trip out to the JFK Museum (overleaf). Begin your evening in a design-driven eaterie such as Banq (see p038), or make a beeline for The Beehive (see p058), a bistro/bar with a diverting cocktail list. For something a bit more Yankee, try the District Restaurant & Lounge (180 Lincoln Street, T 617 426 0180), a SoHo-styled boîte with white leather banquettes and pale, birch-clad walls. *For full addresses, see Resources.*

09.30 Charlie's Sandwich Shoppe

This kind of all-American diner is vanishing from many urban centres. One of the last outposts of old-school authenticity in the luxed-up South End area, the place bills its breakfast as the 'best in America', and it's easy to see why. Served until the 2.30pm closing time, the menu offers a dozen types of omelette, an equal number of fried egg options, pancakes spiked with pecans and raspberries, and an old-fashioned turkey hash. Waist-watchers can opt for egg whites only, but that would mean missing out on half the fun. After all, any eaterie that has been in business since 1927 must be doing something right. Charlie's loyal fan base of hipsters, old-timers and yuppie arrivistes certainly thinks so.

429 Columbus Avenue, T 617 536 7669

12.30 JFK Library & Museum

This IM Pei-designed building contains 20 different exhibitions chronicling the life of John F Kennedy. But if its interiors are informative, the venue is almost as well known for its exterior. Set over 3.85 hectares on the banks of Columbia Point Peninsula, the complex is composed of a nine-storey tower, a pair of auditoriums in an adjoining duplex base and an 11-storey memorial pavilion displaying archival footage and documents from JFK's life. Most of the library is clad with panels that were crafted in nearby North Wibraham, before being hand-fitted on site during construction. Opened in 1979, the complex gained a new wing in 1991. Also designed by IM Pei, it is covered in crisp white concrete and houses conference, meeting and storage spaces.

Columbia Point, T 617 514 1600, jfklibrary.org

John F. Kennedy
PRESIDENTIAL LIBRARY AND MUSEUM

14.30 The Butcher Shop

Chef Barbara Lynch's Butcher Shop is a lower-key version of her flagship, No 9 Park (see p048). This is a sunny space with a menu of European-inspired dishes and a great wine list that is mostly served by the glass. This is a place to linger, with walls of windows that are perfect for people-watching. Service is languid but attentive, and the food matches the vibe: hearty dishes such as shiitake mushroom-spiked arugula risotto, and Yankee standards with a twist – try the hot dogs topped with gruyère and served in a cross between a brioche and a baguette. End the afternoon with a platter of cookies and milk. And if you like what you've eaten, the store's heaving with meats and other goodies to take home.
552 Tremont Street, T 617 423 4800, thebutchershopboston.com

16.00 Barbara Krakow Gallery

Although its location on posh Newbury Street puts it a world away from Boston's more cutting-edge art scene in the South End, the Barbara Krakow Gallery is widely considered to be among the best art spaces in town. Displaying everything from paintings to photographs, drawings and prints, Krakow stocks a blue-chip roster of artists, including Vik Muniz, Jenny Holzer, Dan Flavin and Josef Albers.

This is also the place for expertly curated rotating exhibitions featuring big names such as Julian Opie (pictured). *10 Newbury Street, T 617 262 4490, barbarakrakowgallery.com*

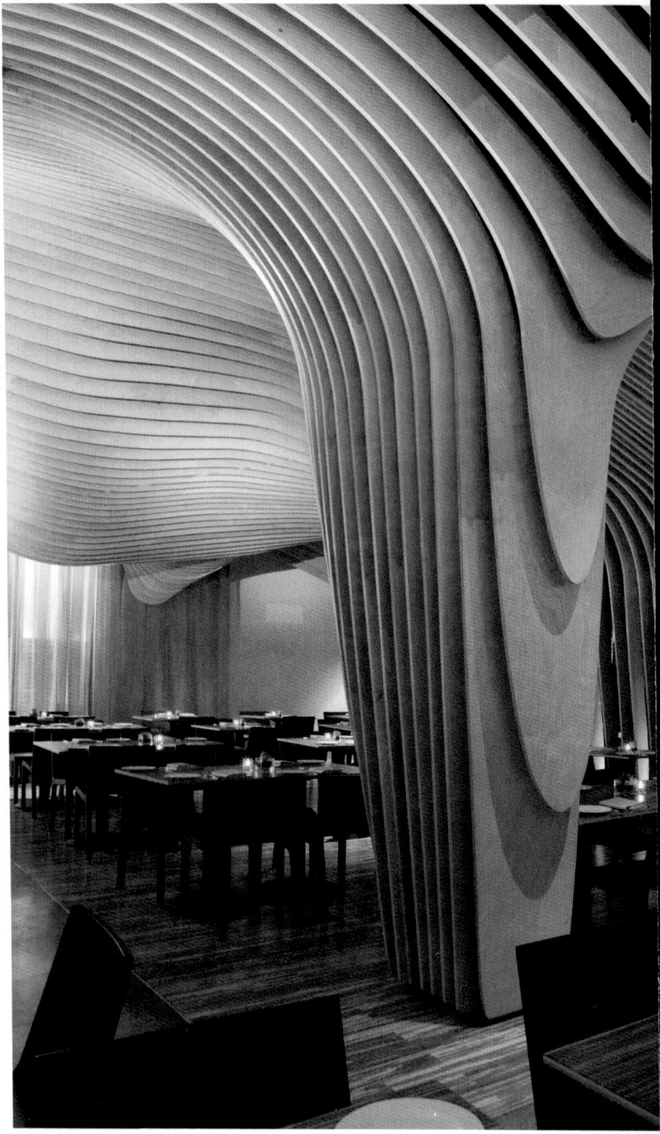

20.00 Banq

Housed behind the 1917 façade of the former Penny Savings Bank, Banq's interiors are a riot of organic shapes and materials that evoke a mix of worldliness and formality. This uniquely undulating space was created by the Boston-based architect team of Monica Ponce de Leon and Nader Tehrani, the brains behind local firm Office dA. Hundreds of curved layers of birch envelop the space to form an abstract canopy above the dining room. Meanwhile, the environmentally friendly tables and high-backed booths are crafted from Plyboo – a form of pressed and recycled bamboo. As for the food, chef Ranveer Brar's menu spans India, Vietnam, Thailand and France, and is executed with ingredients that are both local and global in origin.
1375 Washington Street, T 617 451 0077, banqrestaurant.com

URBAN LIFE
CAFÉS, RESTAURANTS, BARS AND NIGHTCLUBS

At a time when most American cities have fallen prey to suburban sprawl, Boston has retained a true urban feel. Relatively compact, and hemmed in by water on three sides, the city has suceeded in keeping its best features close at hand. Its other great advantage is the arrival each year of tens of thousands of newcomers who flood into the city as students or professionals. This provides a constant groundswell of fresh ideas and inspiration that is reflected in Boston's restaurants, bars and clubs. The best of these major in laid-back luxury, in contrast to the more frenetic vibe in New York.

Excellent Italian cooking remains a staple of many of the city's top restaurants thanks to Boston's thriving immigrant community. But there are also plenty of French and contemporary American menus on offer from star chefs, most notably Barbara Lynch. Her No 9 Park (see p048) and Butcher Shop (see p036) have been at the forefront of the city's epicurean evolution, and her latest venture, located in the FP3 complex (348 Congress Street, T 617 695 1806), in up-and-coming Fort Point Channel, combines a bar, Drink, a café, Sportello, and another restaurant, all of the same high standard.

For a great day's culinary tour, start with a hearty breakfast at Panificio (144 Charles Street, T 617 227 4340), follow with a bistro lunch at Aquitaine (see p045), before pasta and grilled meats for dinner at Franklin Café (278 Shawmut Avenue, T 617 350 0010). *For full addresses, see Resources.*

Gaslight

A second home for the South End's burgeoning artistic community, Gaslight is one of Boston's best French eateries, with a buzzy brasserie vibe and elegant décor. The aesthetic is accented by the hand-crafted zinc bar (from Paris), reclaimed wood flooring, wood-beam ceiling, mosaic tiles and antique mirrors. Gaslight's menu is European to the core: rôtisserie chicken, duck confit, sautéed skate and Niçoise salad. And so is its wine list, which offers more than 20 French vintages. There are daily specials as well as an extensive brunch menu featuring a clutch of hangover-curing cocktails.
560 Harrison Avenue, T 617 422 0224, gaslight560.com

The Achilles Project/Persephone
Boutique by day, restaurant by night, this former fabrics warehouse is the place to go for designer goodies displayed like art, followed by dinner from celebrated local chef Michael Levitan. The menu is big on modern New England dishes – all quaintly sized from 'small' to 'extra large'.
283 Summer Street, T 617 423 2257, achilles-project.com

Clio

Located on the ground floor of The Eliot Hotel (T 617 267 1607), Clio pairs regional American ingredients with traditional French cooking and the occasional Asian touch to create dishes that are both approachable and aspirational. With a 90-seat dining room, it is a bit big to be called cosy, but ivory-coloured chairs and muted beige walls keep it warm and intimate. Co-owner and executive chef Kenneth Oringer graduated 'Most Likely to Succeed' from the Culinary Institute of America – and has more than delivered. Try the frogs' legs sautéed with almonds and wild herbs, or the slow-roasted Kobe steak sweetened with black-fig chutney and organic carrots. Oringer's sashimi and sake bar, Uni, is next door.
The Eliot Hotel, 370 Commonwealth Avenue, T 617 536 7200, cliorestaurant.com

Aquitaine

Owner-chef Seth Woods has gone for Rive Gauche authenticity, with banquettes and leather chairs, mahogany floors and tall windows marking out his Parisian-style bistro. Original French artworks and posters line the walls, as do daily menus featuring Aquitaine classics such as steak frites with black truffle vinaigrette and warm chocolate pudding. There is a great value *prix fixe* weekend brunch and an extensive list of French and Californian wines. With its prime South End location, this is the ideal pit stop in-between shopping sprees. And there is a good sister eaterie – Aquitaine Bis (T 617 734 8400) – in Chestnut Hill. *569 Tremont Street, T 617 424 8577, aquitaineboston.com*

Rialto
A much-loved dining spot in The Charles
Hotel (see p024) near Harvard, Rialto
was given a facelift by its new owner,
chef Jody Adams, in 2007. A focused,
flavoursome Italian menu and lighter
grand dining room emerged to great
applause. Adams also offers regular
classes in Italian regional wines.
1 Bennett Street, T 617 661 5050,
rialto-restaurant.com

No 9 Park

Tucked away in a private townhouse close to the State House (see p064), No 9 Park is an elegant space defined by antique crystal chandeliers, taupe leather banquettes and polished wooden flooring. The buzzy mirrored bar area serves small plates and offers prime Boston Common views, but the main attraction here is the Franco-Italian menu created by chef Barbara Lynch. Be sure to try the prune-stuffed gnocchi with seared foie gras, her signature dish. And savour the wine list by ace sommelier Cat Silirie, which is broadly European, but with excellent American choices. It's well worth taking a chance on the whimsy of Lynch and her local grocers by trying the seven-course tasting menu. *9 Park Street, T 617 742 9991, no9park.com*

Rocca Kitchen & Bar

While Boston has long had a thing for Italian cuisine, few restaurants have taken the genre to such refined levels as Rocca. Located near the new SoWa arts district in the South End, Rocca's soaring, split-level, loft-like home offers a cocktail lounge downstairs and a groovy dining room above. It's all picture windows, peekaboo translucent curtains, walls crafted from brick and cork, and slate-capped tables.

Owner Michela Larson focuses on the cuisine of Liguria in northern Italy, which is best known as the home of pesto. Her team (headed by executive chef Tom Fosnot) pair pesto with trofie pasta, and infuse crisp-skinned seabass with fresh herbs and olives. An inventive selection of pizzas is also on offer.
500 Harrison Avenue, T 617 451 5151, roccaboston.com

B&G Oysters

Opened in 2003, B&G Oysters is another outpost of Barbara Lynch's expanding Boston empire, and specialises in New England seafood classics: perfect lobster rolls, classic *fritto misto* and plates of fresh and fried oysters, all washed down with chilled white wine or sparkling Prosecco. It's all delivered from a central open kitchen ringed by a white marble bar and classic stools. Despite the subterranean location, the restaurant's stainless-steel tiles and pale-blue interiors give B&G a welcome sense of space, as does the cosy garden patio outside. *550 Tremont Street, T 617 423 0550, bandgoysters.com*

Club Café

Boston's key gay restaurant and lounge for 25 years, Club Café is anchored by a long bank of windows that give it a sun-drenched charm during the day. Chef Gery Armsby delivers comfort food with European, Asian and American flavours, such as braised short ribs or sweet-potato gnocchi, before the venue morphs into a late-night cocktail lounge and club. There are nightly DJ sets as well as record- and movie-release parties, and the Sunday brunches are not to be missed – this is when the place feels as welcoming to mature couples as it does to the hip kids.

209 Columbus Avenue, T 617 536 0966, clubcafe.com

O Ya

This restaurant has taken Boston's sushi and sashimi offerings to New York or San Francisco levels, and owner-chef Tim Cushman is not scared to add a touch of Yankee inventiveness to the mix. Fresh lobster comes with *shiso* tempura; foie gras is accented with aged sake; seared diver scallops are paired with foie gras and *shiso*-soaked grapes; and Kumamoto oysters arrive spiked with *yuzu kosho*

aïoli and squid-ink bubbles. O Ya's simple interior is all wood and stone, beneath a towering ceiling. Cushman's wife Nancy put together the sake list, which includes many varieties that are impossible to find elsewhere in New England.
9 East Street, T 617 654 9900,
oyarestaurantboston.com

28 Degrees

Appleton Street is full of Victorian-era buildings with elegant wrought-iron railings. The thoroughly modern 28 Degrees stands out for its dark wooden furniture and colour-saturated lighting. Superb cocktails make this the ideal spot for an after-work get-together or a late-night rendezvous.
1 Appleton Street, T 617 728 0728, 28degrees-boston.com

KO Prime

This stylish steakhouse update in the Nine Zero Hotel (see p020) remains true to its meaty roots. The eclectic dining room has cowhide-covered chairs, antler chandeliers and windows that look onto Boston Common. KO chef Kenneth Oringer of Clio fame (see p044) bases his menu on the finest cuts and fillets, from grass-fed Wagyu and Kobe beef to Kurobuta pork. There is also an extensive list of side dishes, including the must-try pea risotto with lemon and mint. End with the mint mousse dipped in liquid chocolate or a toasted carrot cake. Or come for lunch to try KO's hearty Kobe beefburgers – a luxe take on the American staple. *90 Tremont Street, T 617 772 0202, koprimeboston.com*

People's Republik

Set in the heart of Boston's student mecca, People's Republik is the consummate Cambridge dining and drinking spot, and also one of the few watering holes that stays open until 2am. The place is as welcoming to Harvard types as it is to long-time locals, and the restaurant offers affordable, hearty fare and a generous selection of quality beers. The bar takes its name from Cambridge's traditionally left-leaning vibe and there are Soviet propaganda posters covering its walls. Most of the beers on tap are from local microbreweries, and the dishes include Guinness beef stew and thick-sliced Portobello mushroom sandwiches. The dartboards are perennially popular, and easy-going staff ensure that the atmosphere stays suitably mellow.
876 Massachusetts Avenue, T 617 491 6969

The Beehive

The Cyclorama building, constructed in 1884, was designed to display one huge painting across its cylindrical surface, as was then fashionable. It now houses the Boston Center for the Arts, and in its former boiler room is the busy Beehive. The pan-European menu is good here, as is the jazz, cabaret and burlesque.

541 Tremont Street, T 617 423 0069,
beehiveboston.com

Stix

This indoor/outdoor restaurant/lounge takes its name from the wooden skewers on which many of its edibles are served. Infused with different flavours, the sticks are a cute gimmick that has won this city-centre hot spot a strong following. The dishes themselves are finger foods with grand ideas – bacon and hard-boiled eggs on bourbon-flavoured skewers paired with a maple syrup dipping sauce; foie gras or tuna sashimi on ginger-mango 'stix'; and mussels with lemongrass, coconut and masala. Rhode Island-based design firm 3six0 has given Stix a free and easy feel with cork floors, a liberal use of wood, clever lighting and glow-in-the-dark cube tables in the lounge (above) – making it one of Back Bay's sexiest sipping spots. *35 Stanhope Street, T 617 456 7849, stixboston.com*

INSIDER'S GUIDE

MELISSA WEHRMAN, GRAPHIC DESIGNER

Melissa Wehrman arrived in Boston from Ohio, to work as an art director and now freelance graphic designer. Home is in the South End, an area she loves for its quaint, increasingly arty feel.

Among Boston's many excellent restaurants, she recommends Toro (1704 Washington Street, T 617 536 4300) for tapas – 'order the corn on the cob with Espelette peppers, cheese and lime' – and Douzō (131 Dartmouth Street, T 617 859 8886) in Back Bay for sushi. After dinner, she often heads to the cavernous and buzzy Beehive (see p058) for drinks and live music, or kicks back with a martini at the stylish Pho Republique (1415 Washington Street, T 617 262 0005), a contemporary South-East Asian restaurant and cocktail lounge; 'try the coconut martini'. When Wehrman really wants to let her hair down, she goes to the Middlesex Lounge (315 Massachusetts Avenue, T 617 868 6739) in Cambridge, where the moveable seating allows the dancefloor to expand as the club gets busier. 'The mix of people is always interesting and fun,' she says.

A keen bargain-hunter, Wehrman shops at Filene's Basement (497 Boylston Street, T 617 424 5520), and in summer she likes to rummage around South End Open Market (540 Harrison Avenue, T 617 481 2257), for vintage clothes and jewellery. In the same area, she calls into Parlor (1246-48 Washington Street, T 617 521 9005), a small, independent boutique that sells hard-to-find brands. *For full addresses, see Resources.*

ARCHITOUR

A GUIDE TO BOSTON'S ICONIC BUILDINGS

Boston architecture is rather like the city itself – genteel and historic, but filled with surprises. Dating to literally the dawn of the nation, Bostonian buildings are a dash of old Europe paired with a lot of new America. Although rooted in 17th-century England, Boston's real architectural story begins with Charles Bulfinch – the urban visionary who sought to bring order to the city's then aesthetic chaos. Bulfinch was a traditionalist, and his most important works reflect this sense of nostalgia. His Massachusetts State House (Beacon Street, T 617 727 3676) stands tall as a classic example of colonial-era civic design, reflecting the local élite's desire to align their wealth with the style of their former colonisers.

France, Greece and Italy shaped the city's later architectural evolution, evident in the Haussmann-esque grand boulevards of Back Bay and neo-Gothic/Renaissance/classical monuments, such as Trinity Church (see p013) and Boston Public Library (see p009), around Copley Square and in Fenway. This period of urban expansion delivered Boston into the modern era, when titans such as Le Corbusier, Alvar Aalto and IM Pei left their municipal mark.

More recently, Cambridge – with its flush university duo of MIT and Harvard – has lured high-profile architects. Gehry's Stata Center (opposite and overleaf) is the most famous, but Simmons Hall (see p074) is also a show-stopper and a worthy rival. *For full addresses, see Resources.*

Ray and Maria Stata Center

With its irregular façade and pop-out windows, the 2004 Ray and Maria Stata Center unabashedly displays its Frank Gehry pedigree. Designed by the architect as a home for myriad MIT science laboratories as well as linguistics and philosophy departments, it was funded by the Statas and Bill Gates, among others. The first four floors of the building rise in alignment before branching off into two distinct towers. Covering 67,815 sq m, it flows freely from red brick to mirrored steel, brushed aluminium to corrugated metal. Critics have argued that it feels 'unfinished', but the Stata Center has helped establish MIT as the region's architectural hot spot, stealing a dose of much-needed attention from its more media-savvy neighbour, Harvard.
32 Vassar Street, T 617 253 2600

John Hancock Tower

Rising 241m above Copley Square, IM Pei
and Henry Cobb's soaring tower of thick
black glass looks as fresh and modern
today as it did when it opened in 1976.
It is the tallest building in New England,
and, due to the lack of any surrounding
skyscrapers, wears this title boldly. Clad
in a dark reflective skin, the structure is
a vertical slab of 10,344 glass panes that
seems to capture and project everything
around it. The architects gave the design
a charming twist by shaping the base in the
form of a parallelogram. Although clearly
an architectural triumph, the tower has
been plagued by problems, from falling
glass panels during its construction to
the closure of its celebrated observation
deck following 9/11. It stands in striking
juxtaposition to the nearby 19th-century
Trinity Church (see p013).
200 Clarendon Street, T 617 247 1997

Kresge Auditorium
One of two campus buildings designed
by the Finnish-American architect Eero
Saarinen (the other is the nearby Chapel),
this is the home of the MIT Philharmonic.
The 1955 structure comprises a thin
concrete shell capped by a copper dome
and has no internal support columns.
'Clouds' suspended from the ceiling
were designed to perfect the acoustics.
48 Massachusetts Avenue

The Institute of Contemporary Art

Since opening in December 2006, the waterfront Institute of Contemporary Art has helped secure Fort Point Channel as Boston's HQ of hipness. Designed by New York's Diller Scofidio + Renfro, the ICA is the city's first new museum in almost a century, and it's a stunning, cantilevered glass confection. Two sunlight-suffused galleries totalling 5,760 sq m are joined by a 325 sq m promenade wrapped in a sheath of glass. On display are grand pieces from the permanent collection (from Nan Goldin to Louise Bourgeois) and monthly temporary exhibitions. The money shot is the Poss Family Mediatheque – a novel digital media centre that seemingly pushes visitors towards the waves below.
100 Northern Avenue, T 617 478 3100, icaboston.org

Simmons Hall

It may be simple student digs, but it's fair to say that MIT's 2002 Simmons Hall is the most compellingly designed dormitory in America. The work of New York's Steven Holl Architects and Perry Dean Rogers Architects, its aluminium skin is punctuated by more than 5,500 windows (nine in each dorm room), with dining, meeting and theatre spaces all flowing through a dramatic 116m-long structure. Five main porticoes, which Holl describes as both walkways and the hall's 'lungs', help the movement of air and light through the space. The hall is a blend of unexpected voids and grand cantilevers linked to a solid base, and, when illuminated at night, it forms a spectacular fluid-like grid.
229 Vassar Street, T 617 253 5107,
simmons.mit.edu

One International Place

Completed in 1987, One International Place is the fifth-tallest building in the city and part of the larger 167,225 sq m International Place complex. Designed by Philip Johnson and John Burgee, the structures bring to mind New York's World Financial Center or London's Docklands – a cluster of towers capped by triangular and circular roofs. One International Place rises 180m to 46 floors, crafted from mostly rose-tinted rough granite paired with a curtain of aluminium and punctuated by numerous Palladian windows – a signature postmodern touch by Johnson. A pair of smaller, though similarly designed, structures were later built alongside the tower.
100 Oliver Street

Leonard P Zakim Bunker Hill Bridge

Built as a major component of the Big Dig project, the Leonard P Zakim Bunker Hill crossing is the widest cable-stayed bridge in the world, at 56m, and was named after a local civil rights activist. It forms part of Interstate 93 and US Route 1 and replaced an often jammed six-lane highway that closed in 1999 and was eventually pulled down in 2004. The new, £56.1m, eight-lane structure is defined by a pair of sail-like, 82m towers, designed by the Swiss bridge specialist Christian Menn, and opened in 2003. Stretching alongside it is the four-lane Leverett Circle Connector Bridge, and together they have more than doubled traffic capacity. Just below, 16 hectares of riverbank have been freed up and are being redeveloped as parkland.
leonardpzakimbunkerhillbridge.org

Carpenter Center for the Visual Arts
Harvard's visual arts hub is America's
only building designed by Le Corbusier.
However, the Swiss-born architect never
actually set foot on site during its design
or construction (it was completed in 1963),
as he was confined to his home in Paris
due to ill health. The project was managed
instead by José Luis Sert, the then dean
of Harvard's Graduate School of Design.
The final cost was £820,000 – a fantastic
sum for a structure of such modesty.
But what a structure it is. Listed on
America's National Register of Historic
Places, it is a seamless blend of concrete
shell and slim columns, cast in concrete
masonry and dominated by a curved
ramp. The centre houses the Department
of Visual and Environmental Studies,
the Harvard Film Archive, and two public
galleries that put on regular exhibitions.
24 Quincy Street, ves.fas.harvard.edu

SHOPPING

THE BEST RETAIL THERAPY AND WHAT TO BUY

Over the past few years, Boston's shopping culture has achieved world-class status, with top-tier retailers ranging from Barneys (100 Huntington Avenue, T 617 385 3300) to Marc Jacobs (81 Newbury Street, T 617 425 0707) opening outposts. Much of this maturity follows from the city's still-expanding economy, with wealth created by a boom in financial services and high-tech sectors. Most choice boutiques are located in Back Bay, mainly on Newbury Street. At its eastern end stands the venerable Louis Boston (234 Berkeley Street, T 800 225 5135), with its elegant new-Venetian architecture and choice of global labels. Nearby is Alan Bilzerian (34 Newbury Street, T 617 536 1001), offering an expertly edited selection of European brands. However, the arrival of big-box stores such as H&M (100 Newbury Street, T 617 859 3192) is causing some to worry about Newbury's luxe longevity.

Away from Back Bay, the South End and Beacon Hill also offer compelling retail therapy. Both focus more on small-scale, independent boutiques selling quality crafted clothing, furniture or chichi home accessories. Beacon Hill's smartest stores are anchored along Charles Street and – owing to the area's centuries of history – have a more patrician, frou-frou feel. In the South End, and particularly around Union Park, the vibe is more cutting edge, although still with a fine eye for craftsmanship.

For full addresses, see Resources.

Ars Libri

Unusually for a bookstore in a prime city-centre spot, Ars Libri presents a world of recherché books specialising in art, design, architecture and photography. Its focus on rare and out-of-print titles, along with monographs and reference publications, makes it a treasure trove for scholars; in fact, it is the largest collection of its kind in America. Since 1976, the shop has been a lifeline for its fans, who rely on the keen eye of owner Elmar W Seibel. He will help track down even the most elusive items, and his catalogues are works of art in themselves. Ars Libri recently joined forces with the Museum of Fine Arts (see p009) to offer curated book displays in conjunction with exhibitions being held at the museum.
500 Harrison Avenue, T 617 357 5212, arslibri.com

Uniform

Set where posh Back Bay meets the hipper South End, Uniform targets men of all ages with a funky collection of mainly casual and streetwear. Opened in 2005 by Gary Ritacco, it stocks easy-to-wear brands such as Penguin, Victorinox and Ben Sherman. There are Gola trainers, bags by Freitag (a Boston exclusive), scents by Comme des Garçons and treats by The Art of Shaving – all housed in the sleek Atelier 505 building. With his keen eye, not to mention a winning personality, Ritacco will help even the most fashion-challenged create total looks. There is also an array of unisex items, including indulgent goodies by Korres. Ask nicely and Uniform will deliver to hotels and apartments around the South End.
511 Tremont Street, T 617 247 2360, uniformboston.com

Hudson

This tiny boutique is one of a plethora of independents helping establish the South End as Boston's mecca of hip. Owner Jill Goldberg is a one-time struggling West Coast actress who now purveys her own eclectic taste in homewares and elegant bric-a-brac. Her stock includes vintage pieces as well as regional furniture and accessories, such as sofas by Shabby Chic, art deco-influenced lamps from Worlds Away and rugs by Dash & Albert Rug Company. Look out too for Hudson's own-brand cushions, made from rare vintage feed bags; a selection of artisanal chocolates; and a range of kids' goods, including recycled cotton blankets.
312 Shawmut Avenue, T 617 292 0900, hudsonboston.com

Plum Produce
This small-scale greengrocer and demo kitchen is another part of Barbara Lynch's sprawling culinary empire. Located moments from her B&G Oysters (see p050) and The Butcher Shop (see p036), Plum Produce stocks fresh delights from local farms, plus pickled vegetables, dried fruits and chocolates. *106 Waltham Street, T 617 423 7586, plumproduce.com*

Montage

No shop in the city can compete with Montage when it comes to contemporary furniture. The sprawling showroom stocks an extensive range of global brands, many of which are Boston exclusives, in a sun-drenched space. Founded in 1959 by Albert W Sylvester and Howell A Bates, it is still run by Bates' son Chris, a regular presence at global design shows, and brings to Boston Italian masters such as B&B Italia, Cassina, Poltrona Frau and Fiam Italia. American designers are in favour too, including Marc Desplaines, whose hand-crafted designs for Antoine Proulx are a speciality. The store sponsors numerous local design events, including the Montage/Arclinea Contemporary Design Scholarship Competition.
75 Arlington Street, T 617 451 9400, montageweb.com

Envi

Eco-conscious fashion is a good idea, but often comes up short on style and substance. Which is why Envi was so welcome when it showed up on Newbury Street during the spring of 2007. Owners Callie Smith and Ursula Stahl declared upon its debut that Envi was committed to making eco-sensitive clothing 'hip not hippy'. The duo were clearly serious, stocking their shelves with brands such as denim label Del Forte, Stewart + Brown and Twice Shy – all with design values that are as exemplary as their green credentials. Items are crafted from organically grown, sustainable fabrics such as cotton, hemp and a soybean-derived fibre touted as a veggie alternative to cashmere.
164 Newbury Street, T 617 267 3684, shopenvi.com

SPORTS AND SPAS

WORK OUT, CHILL OUT OR JUST WATCH

Considering the fact that it's very cold for half the year, it's no great surprise that many of Boston's athletic pursuits take place indoors. Whether it's a basketball game or a yoga class, Bostonians rely on heated venues to enjoy the action or get in shape. Still, they take their physical fitness seriously, and snow is not always a deterrent. Joggers head to the Charles River promenade, rowers take to the water, and cyclists make the most of the relatively flat terrain.

Boston's proximity to numerous snow-capped New England peaks means some top-notch skiing is just a short drive away. In Vermont, the runs at Stowe, which you can reach by car in under two hours, stay powder-packed into late spring. Further north, Sugarloaf is one of Maine's most popular ski areas, while in New Hampshire, Mount Sunapee makes for a great day trip.

Back in town, the major sporting draws are the Boston Celtics basketball and Red Sox baseball teams. The latter plays in the warmer months in Fenway Park (opposite), which is the oldest Major League stadium in America. There's also the New England Patriots American football team, whose star player, Tom Brady, has given the sport a new sense of cool. Most of the big events attract massive crowds and several of the city's top-tier hotels offer game-based packages, though any concierge worth his or her salt should be able to secure some coveted last-minute tickets.

For full addresses, see Resources.

Fenway Park

The home of the Red Sox is the place to experience that most American of pastimes – a game of baseball. Boston is a serious sports town, and if the Red Sox are the pulse of the city, Fenway Park is its symbolic heart, having hosted 10 World Series. The stadium opened in 1912 and has retained its original design and wooden seats. Over the past few years, it has also begun luring non-sports fans, with high-profile concerts in late August and early September. While the stadium remains a quaint testament to an earlier era, financial pressure on its owners is likely to see it grow dramatically to accommodate up to 45,000 seats by 2015.
*Kenmore Square, 4 Yawkey Way,
T 617 226 6666*

Exhale Mind Body Spa

The most central and chic spa in town is ideal for those who want an active as well as a relaxing experience, with core, yoga and Pilates sessions offered alongside skin and body treatments, nutritional advice, acupuncture and detox programmes in a 1,200 sq m space overlooking the Public Garden. Designed by Studios Architecture in 2004, Exhale is airy and light-filled, with a signature yoga studio (left) that has a temple-like aesthetic, and 15 treatment rooms, each finished in a Zen-like palette of earthy greens, white and beige. The signature one-hour Body Enlightenment treatment incorporates yoga techniques, assisted stretching and body alignment, and is designed to rebalance physically and mentally. The recently developed organic skincare line GRN (Grow Restore Nurture) is excellent.
28 Arlington Street, T 617 532 7000, exhalespa.com

TD Banknorth Garden
This 1995 stadium by architects Ellerbe
Becket is best known as the home of
the Boston Celtics basketball team. The
Bruins ice hockey team also play here,
and the venue hosts pop concerts and
graduation ceremonies. Some 3.5 million
people pass through annually, though
none are as fanatical as the Celtics fans.
100 Legends Way, T 617 624 1050,
tdbanknorthgarden.com

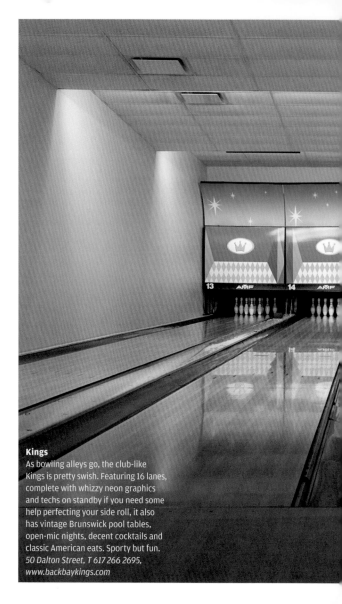

Kings
As bowling alleys go, the club-like Kings is pretty swish. Featuring 16 lanes, complete with whizzy neon graphics and techs on standby if you need some help perfecting your side roll, it also has vintage Brunswick pool tables, open-mic nights, decent cocktails and classic American eats. Sporty but fun.
50 Dalton Street, T 617 266 2695, www.backbaykings.com

ESCAPES

WHERE TO GO IF YOU WANT TO LEAVE TOWN

From Boston it is an easy drive to ultra-scenic Cape Cod (overleaf), the location of popular summer vacation destinations such as Martha's Vineyard, Provincetown and Nantucket. Away from the coast lie the classic getaways of the Berkshire Mountains, such as Tanglewood (297 West Street, Lenox, T 413 637 1600), which is home to the Boston Symphony Orchestra. The Berkshires are also winning a reputation for world-class contemporary art (see p100) and architecture, especially since the advent of Tadao Ando's characteristically understated concrete-and-glass addition to the Stone Hill Center (225 South Street, Williamstown, T 413 458 2303).

To the north of Boston lies New Hampshire, where the rugged Atlantic coastline provides a home for historic communities such as Portsmouth Harbor and its (reputedly) haunted lighthouse. Landlocked and liberal, neighbouring Vermont is beloved for its rolling hills, ski runs and foodie scene, which includes some 30 boutique cheese-makers. Sample the products at Hen of the Wood (92 Stowe Street, Waterbury, T 802 244 7300), or check out New England culinary favourites such as flan with Maine sweetcorn at the revamped Inn at Ocean's Edge (24 Stonecoast Road, T 207 236 0945), just outside Camden. In Rhode Island, the waterfront town of Newport is still renowned for the monumental mansions that were built by the titans of America's industrial age.

For full addresses, see Resources.

DeCordova Museum, Lincoln

This world-class museum and sculpture park is located in the quaint New England town of Lincoln, 25km west of Boston. Although the museum is mainly dedicated to contemporary art, its setting could not be more traditional – a renovated mansion dating from the early 1900s surrounded by a lake and expansive woodlands. The park was founded in 1948 and has since amassed an impressive collection, including pieces by artists such as Jim Dine, Alexander Calder and Sol LeWitt. On offer are guided tours, a tempting café, and a shop stocking original artworks, jewellery and educational toys.
51 Sandy Pond Road, T 781 259 8355, decordova.org

Airplane House, Cape Cod

Designed by William Gray Purcell and George Grant Elmslie, this 1911 Prairie Style house takes its name from its unusual shape, formed along a central axis flanked by two symmetrical wings and headed by a semicircular living space. Equally distinctive for its broad, flat roofs, the building is perched on the edge of a peninsula in Woods Hole and boasts super ocean views through its numerous windows. Following a 30-year renovation, the property is now available for summer rental (T 508 548 0703). Interior highlights include the 92 stained-glass windows, each of which feature a unique geometric pattern, and the upstairs bedrooms, which have been restored to their original state and feature fittings and textiles designed by Purcell and Elmslie.
Juniper Point, Woods Hole

MASS MoCA, Berkshire Mountains
Opened in 1999, MASS MoCA is the largest contemporary arts and cultural centre in the US, with 19 galleries spread over a 9,300 sq m site in the Berkshire Mountains, about 2.5 hours east of Boston. A one-time textiles factory, most of the museum's buildings date from the second half of the 19th century. Expertly renovated by architects Bruner/Cott & Associates, the site is now listed on the National Register of Historic Places and is credited with helping revive the economy of the region. Inside, the museum's vast spaces permit the display of large-scale works by artists such as Anselm Kiefer (*Étroits sont les vaisseaux*, above) and Fransje Killaars. MASS MoCA holds regular arts events, from music concerts to film festivals.
87 Marshall Street, North Adams, T 413 662 2111, massmoca.org

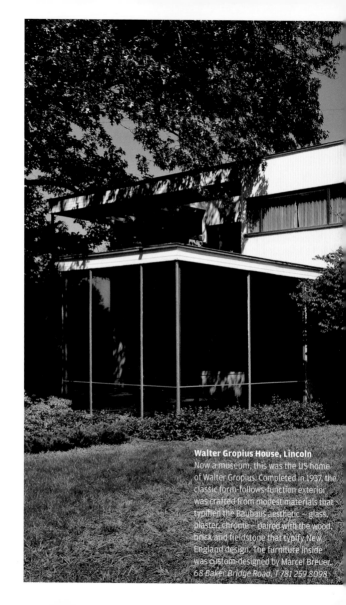

Walter Gropius House, Lincoln
Now a museum, this was the US home
of Walter Gropius. Completed in 1937, the
classic form-follows-function exterior
was crafted from modest materials that
typified the Bauhaus aesthetic – glass,
plaster, chrome – paired with the wood,
brick and fieldstone that typify New
England design. The furniture inside
was custom-designed by Marcel Breuer.
68 Baker Bridge Road, T 781 259 8098

NOTES
SKETCHES AND MEMOS

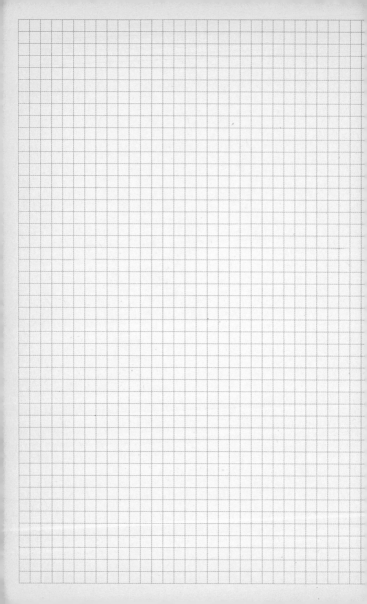

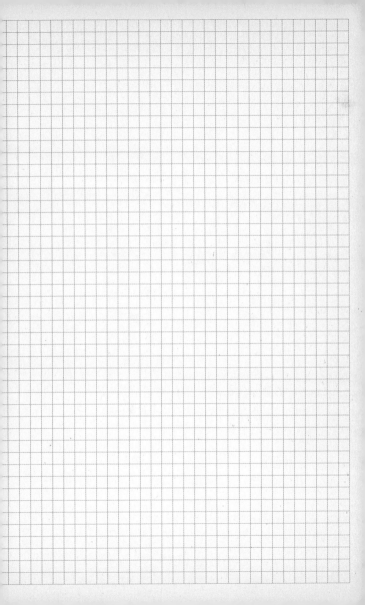

RESOURCES

CITY GUIDE DIRECTORY

HOTELS

ADDRESSES AND ROOM RATES

Airplane House 098
Room rates:
weekly rental, prices on request
Juniper Point
Woods Hole
Cape Cod
T 508 548 0703

The Beacon Hill Hotel 030
Room rates:
double, from $245;
Jacobs Suite, from $365
25 Charles Street
T 617 723 7575
beaconhillhotel.com

The Charles Hotel 024
Room rates:
double, $335
1 Bennett Street
T 617 864 1200
charleshotel.com

Clarendon Square Inn 026
Room rates:
double, from $175;
Clarendon Suite, from $340
198 W Brookline Street
T 617 536 2229
clarendonsquare.com

The Eliot Hotel 044
Room rates:
double, from $290
370 Commonwealth Avenue
T 617 267 1607
eliothotel.com

The Fairmont Copley Plaza 017
Room rates:
double, from $325;
Presidential Suite, from $4,500
138 St James Avenue
T 617 267 5300
fairmont.com/copleyplaza

XV Beacon 022
Room rates:
double, from $330;
Studio Room, from $470
15 Beacon Street
T 617 670 1500
xvbeacon.com

Four Seasons 016
Room rates:
double, from $480;
Executive Suite Garden View, $1,000
200 Boylston Street
T 617 338 4400
fourseasons.com/boston

Inn at Ocean's Edge 096
Room rates:
double, from $195
24 Stonecoast Road
Lincolnville
Maine
T 207 236 0945
innatoceansedge.com

InterContinental 021
  Room rates:
  double, from $250;
  Superior Suite, from $2,250
  510 Atlantic Avenue
  T 617 747 1000
  intercontinentalboston.com

The Liberty Hotel 018
  Room rates:
  double, from $550;
  original jail rooms, from $750
  215 Charles Street
  T 617 224 4000
  libertyhotel.com

Mandarin Oriental 016
  Room rates:
  double, from $725
  776 Boylston Street
  T 617 535 8888
  mandarinoriental.com/boston

Nine Zero Hotel 020
  Room rates:
  Deluxe, from $410;
  Premier, from $440;
  Premier with View, from $490;
  Cloud Nine Penthouse Suite, from $3,935
  90 Tremont Street
  T 617 772 5800
  ninezero.com

Renaissance 016
  Room rates:
  double, from $300
  606 Congress Street
  T 617 338 4111
  marriott.com

The Ritz-Carlton 028
  Room rates:
  double, from $625;
  Luxury Park View Suite, from $3,500;
  Presidential Suite, $5,625
  10 Avery Street
  T 617 574 7100
  ritzcarlton.com

Taj 016
  Room rates:
  double, from $550
  15 Arlington Street
  T 617 536 5700
  tajhotels.com/boston

Westin 016
  Room rates:
  double, $480
  425 Summer Street
  T 617 532 4600
  starwoodhotels.com

WALLPAPER* CITY GUIDES

Editorial Director
Richard Cook

Art Director
Loran Stosskopf
Editor
Rachael Moloney
Author
David Kaufman
Deputy Editor
Jeremy Case
Managing Editor
Jessica Diamond

Chief Designer
Daniel Shrimpton
Designer
Lara Collins

Map Illustrator
Russell Bell

Photography Editor
Sophie Corben
Photography Assistant
Robin Key

Sub-Editors
Melanie Parr
Julian Satterthwaite
Editorial Assistant
Ella Marshall

Interns
Rosa Bertoli
Dan Lewis

**Wallpaper* Group
Editor-in-Chief**
Tony Chambers
Publishing Director
Gord Ray

Contributors
Sara Henrichs
Meirion Pritchard
Ellie Stathaki

Wallpaper* ® is a
registered trademark
of IPC Media Limited

All prices are correct at
time of going to press,
but are subject to change.

PHAIDON

Phaidon Press Limited
Regent's Wharf
All Saints Street
London N1 9PA

Phaidon Press Inc
180 Varick Street
New York, NY 10014

Phaidon® is a registered
trademark of Phaidon
Press Limited

www.phaidon.com

First published 2009
© 2009 IPC Media Limited

ISBN 978 0 7148 4895 2

A CIP Catalogue record for
this book is available from
the British Library.

Printed in China

PHOTOGRAPHERS

BOSTON

A COLOUR-CODED GUIDE TO THE HOT 'HOODS

CAMBRIDGE
Home to Harvard and MIT, this is also an upmarket district of elegant colonial-era houses

DOWNTOWN
Skyscrapers, landmark buildings and a chaotic Chinatown make up Boston's bustling heart

FORT POINT CHANNEL
Once forgotten, now booming, this former warehouse zone has seen an influx of cool

FENWAY
No, not just the Red Sox – there's fine art, contemporary architecture and kicking clubs

BACK BAY
Bourgeois boulevards evoke Hausmann, but the shopping is falling prey to big brands

SOUTH END
This multicultural enclave is packed with independent boutiques and hip restaurants

BEACON HILL
A haven for the city's élite, who flash their cash in the swanky stores on Charles Street

NORTH END
The birthplace of Boston can boast historic sites and the myriad eateries of Little Italy

For a full description of each neighbourhood, see the Introduction.
Featured venues are colour-coded, according to the district in which they are located.